How to Create Language Experts With
Literary Terms

Codi Hrouda and Emma McInerney
with Lyle Lee Jenkins

My Book of Connecting Themes to Real Events

By: _____

School: _____

Teacher: _____

Date: _____

My Second Book of Judging Actual Events

By: _____

School: _____

Teacher: _____

Date: _____

My Book of Latin Roots

By: _____

School: _____

Teacher: _____

Date: _____

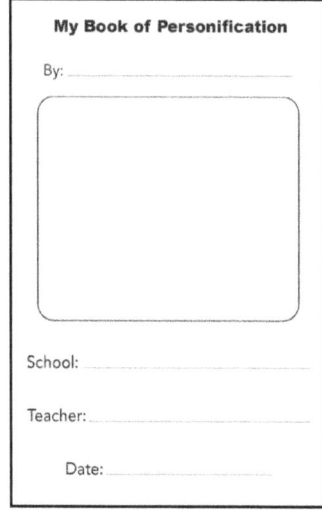

My Book of Personification

By: _____

School: _____

Teacher: _____

Date: _____

My Book of Idioms

By: _____

School: _____

Teacher: _____

Date: _____

Perfect School Collection™

Copyright © 2023 by Codi Hrouda, Emma McInerney and Lyle Lee Jenkins

All rights reserved. No part of this publication may be reproduced, distributed, or transmitted in any form or by any means, including photocopying, recording, or other electronic or mechanical methods, without the prior written permission of the publisher, LtoJ Press, except in the case of brief quotations embodied in critical reviews and certain other non-commercial uses permitted by copyright law.

To contact the authors regarding keynotes, workshops or bulk orders, visit LtoJ.net/Contact

ISBN: 978-1-956457-70-4

Book Design & Graphics: Christy Courtright, Christy's Customs LLC
Quality Assurance Manager: Kelly Lippert
Publishing Consultant: Martha Bullen, Bullen Publishing Services
Distribution Coordinator: Maggie McLaughlin

Printed in the United States of America

The Perfect School Collection™

How to Create a Perfect School by Lyle Lee Jenkins
How to Create a Perfect Home School by Lyle Lee Jenkins and Kelly Hawkinson Lippert

Perfect School Collection™ Resources

How to Create Math Experts series by Peggy McLean and Lyle Lee Jenkins
How to Create Math Experts with Fluency Quizzes by Peggy McLean and Lyle Lee Jenkins
How to Create Math Experts with Math Standards Quizzes by Peggy McLean, Laura Hayes and Lyle Lee Jenkins
How to Create a Math Foundation for Future Math Experts by Lyle Lee Jenkins
How to Create Bible Experts: Genesis to Revelation by Richard Douglas Junior Jenkins with Lyle Lee Jenkins

Early Readers

Bible Patterns for Young Readers series by Lyle Lee Jenkins
Aesop Patterns for Young Readers series by Lyle Lee Jenkins

Young Authors

Wordless Books for Young Authors series by Jim Chansler and Lyle Lee Jenkins

Special Project

All About Henry: Rich Widower of Savannah Valley by Lyle Lee Jenkins

CONTENTS

Purchasers of *How to Create Language Experts with Literary Terms* may utilize the QR code provided at the end of the book to download student booklets from this book at no extra cost. Both the print and downloaded copies are protected by copyright laws.

INTRODUCTION

The philosophy behind these booklets is that they are student-led, and elementary (K - 6) standards driven. In other words, students can independently complete much of the materials they are expected to learn in school with occasional pre-teaching.

The booklets are designed with a left-brain/right-brain balance. The back cover is a right-brain activity and the inside pages are clearly left-brain. The page prior to each grade level gives parents and teachers background knowledge and suggestions to successfully support their students and children through the booklets.

In order to create and assemble the booklets, parents and teachers can scan the QR code provided at the end of the book to download digital copies. To ensure proper printing, please utilize double sided printing and set your printer to "flip" on the short edge. The front page will be the front and back cover of the booklet. We have also included some bonus booklets within this series to support additional literary term exploration.

Enjoy,

Codi Hrouda, Emma McInerney and Lyle Lee Jenkins

GRADE 5
BOOKLET DIRECTIONS

My Book of Homonyms:
Students may need to be pre-taught homonyms. Access to coloring supplies will be needed for this booklet.

My Book of Comparing and Contrasting Settings:
Students will need to have access to a literary book that contains flashbacks or flash forwards that change the time period or place.

My Book of Connecting Themes to Real Events:
Students will need to have access to two literary books.

Detective: What Does This Author Really Think?
Students will need to have access to two opinion texts (current event articles, blog posts, comic strips, etc.).

My Second Book of Judging Actual Events:
Students will need to have access to a historical fiction and non-fiction book on the same topic and coloring supplies for this booklet.

My Book of Latin Roots:
Students may need to be pre-taught root words and given examples.

My Book of Alliteration:
Students may need to be pre-taught alliteration and given examples. Access to a variety of text such as: articles, song lyrics, comic books and coloring supplies will be needed for this booklet.

My Book of Personification:
Students may need to be pre-taught personification and given examples. Access to coloring supplies will be needed for this booklet.

My Book of Idioms:
Students may need to be pre-taught idioms and given examples. Access to a variety of text such as: articles, song lyrics, comic books and coloring supplies will be needed for this booklet.

My Book of Hyperboles:
Students may need to be pre-taught hyperbole and given examples.

Create silly sentences using homonym pairs in each sentence:

_____

_____

_____

_____

_____

_____

_____

_____

_____

My Book of Homonyms

By: _____

School: _____

Teacher: _____

Date: _____

Homonyms - two or more words with the **same spelling and pronunciation** but **different meanings.**
Example: Tie - to band together, Tie - article of clothing worn around the neck.

Draw a picture for each homonym pair to show the two different meanings.

Fall

Rose

Write a sentence for each homonym to show both meanings:

Quarter
Sentence 1:

_____

_____

Sentence 2:

_____

_____

Bank
Sentence 1:

_____

_____

Sentence 2:

_____

_____

Student booklets are available via the QR code at the end of the book

Write a story with the same setting (time and place) but a different plot as your most recent read.

_____

_____

_____

_____

_____

_____

_____

_____

_____

My Book of Comparing and Contrasting Setting

By: _____

School: _____

Teacher: _____

Date: _____

Read a fictional book and compare and contrast the setting (time period and place) within the book.

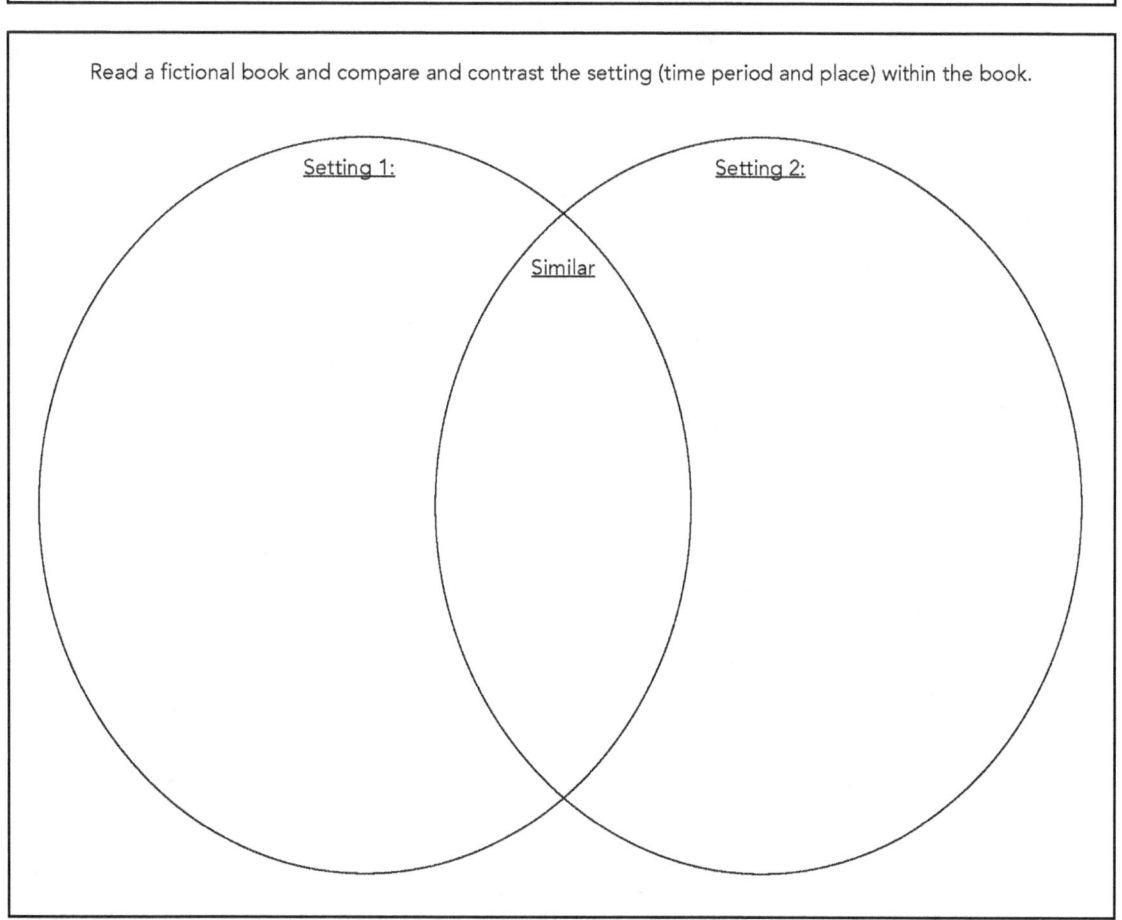

Setting 1:

Setting 2:

Similar

Student booklets are available via the QR code at the end of the book

Write a realistic fiction story that has the same theme as one of the books you've read:

My Book of Connecting Themes to Real Events

By: _____

School: _____

Teacher: _____

Date: _____

_____

_____

_____

_____

_____

_____

_____

_____

Read two fictional books and identify their theme. Then write about a time when you have experienced each theme in your life.

_____
Title of Book 1

_____
Title of Book 2

Theme:

_____

_____

_____

Real-World Connection:

_____

_____

_____

Theme:

_____

_____

_____

Real-World Connection:

_____

_____

_____

Student booklets are available via the QR code at the end of the book

After reading both opinion texts, which text do you side with? Explain why.

_____

_____

_____

_____

_____

_____

_____

_____

_____

_____

Detective: What Does This Author Really Think?

By: _____

School: _____

Teacher: _____

Date: _____

Read two opinion texts that have different perspectives on the same topic. While reading, write down the author's belief and evidence that supports their opinion.

Title of Text 1	Title of Text 2
Author's Belief:	Author's Belief:
Evidence:	Evidence:

Student booklets are available via the QR code at the end of the book

Research an important event in American history, Create a book cover representing the details of the historical event.

My Second Book of Judging Actual Events

By: _____

School: _____

Teacher: _____

Date: _____

Read a literary and a non-fiction book on the same topic. In the chart below, fill in events/facts as you read. Once you are done reading cross out any literary events/facts that were not repeated in the non-fiction book.

Literary Book Title	Non-Fiction Book Title

Student booklets are available via the QR code at the end of the book

Research more Latin roots. Then choose one to create a diagram that displays the root word with all the possible prefixes and suffixes that can be applied.

My Book of Latin Roots

By: _____

School: _____

Teacher: _____

Date: _____

Latin Roots - a word with a Latin origin that does not have a prefix or suffix, but one can be added to change the meaning of the word.
Example: root - audi, audience

Match the following Latin roots with their meanings

List as many related words as you can find for each Latin root:

port	ject
dict	pend

Form
(transform format)

A. to draw or pull

Tract
(attract, subtract)

B. to look

Spect
(inspect, spectator)

C. to shape

Act
(action, actor)

D. to act or do

Create and illustrate two silly alliterations:

My Book of Alliterations

By: _____

School: _____

Teacher: _____

Date: _____

Alliteration - the repetition of the same sound at the beginning of a sequence of words.
Example: **C**indy **S**wam in the **S**wimming Pool.

Read a variety of text (song lyrics, articles, comic books, etc.) and list as many examples of alliterations as you can find.

Text	Alliteration
_____	_____
_____	_____
_____	_____
_____	_____
_____	_____
_____	_____
_____	_____
_____	_____

Read each sentence and underline the words that create an alliteration:

1. Mary made mouth-watering muffins on Monday.

2. Andrea ate apples all day.

3. Soft snow falls silently.

4. The tornado tossed the turtle into the tree.

Choose or create a personification and draw both the literal and figurative meanings

My Book of Personification

By: _____

School: _____

Teacher: _____

Date: _____

Personification - giving human qualities to animals or objects.

Read each sentence and underline the word or phrase that personifies the animal or objects.
Example: The **stars winked** at me.

1. The last piece of cake was calling my name.

2. The plant was begging for water.

3. The wind whistled through the trees.

4. Lighting danced across the sky.

Add a phrase to the objects below that best personifies them.

The sun _____

_____

My alarm clock _____

_____

The thunder _____

_____

Her balloon _____

_____

Idioms are often used to describe real-life situations. Research the meaning of the following three idioms:

"don't judge a book by its cover"
"Rome wasn't built in a day"
"the end doesn't justify the means"

Then choose one of those idioms to write about a real-world connection you've experienced.

_____

_____

_____

_____

_____

_____

_____

_____

_____

My Book of Idioms

By: _____

School: _____

Teacher: _____

Date: _____

Idiom - a phrase that means something different from its literal meaning.
Example: Easy does it = slow down

For each idiom, draw pictures that show the literal meaning and the figurative meaning.

All in the same boat.

Letting the cat out of the bag.

Read a variety of texts (song lyrics, articles, comic books, etc.) to find multiple idioms. List them in the chart below and state their figurative meaning.

Idiom	Figurative Meaning
_____	_____
_____	_____
_____	_____
_____	_____
_____	_____
_____	_____
_____	_____
_____	_____
_____	_____

Write a poem using multiple examples of hyperboles.

My Book of Hyperboles

By: _____

School: _____

Teacher: _____

Date: _____

Hyperbole - an exaggerated statement.
Example: Dying of laughter.

Match each phrase with its corresponding hyperbole:

The man was so hungry he could...   A. a mile wide

Her smile was...   B. as a toothpick

I am so confused my head...   C. sleep for a year

He is as skinny...   D. eat a horse

She was so tired she could...   E. is spinning

Replace the words in parenthesis with a hyperbole
Write the new sentence on the line below.

I have (a lot) of things to do today.

_____

My dog is (large).

_____

His homework took (a long time) to complete.

_____

It is raining (hard).

_____

CONTINUE CREATING LITERARY EXPERTS

BONUS BOOKLETS

A quick internet search for literary terms brings up hundreds of words. In addition, there are many topics to study as students gain more meaning from language and increase their writing skills.

Thus, the following blank pages are designed for students to write additional booklets about literary terms not included in *How to Create Language Experts with Literary Terms*. After selecting a new term, students select the format that best fits the task of writing about the literary term or concept.

There are times when children become so engrossed with a particular term that they want to make their booklet larger. These blank pages can also be used to add to existing booklets included in *How to Create Language Experts with Literary Terms*.

Student booklets are available via the QR code at the end of the book

My Book of _____

By: _____

School: _____

Teacher: _____

Date: _____

_____
Title of Book 1

_____
Title of Book 2

Student booklets are available via the QR code at the end of the book

My art:

Student booklets are available via the QR code at the end of the book

Book 1 Title: _____   Book 2 Title: _____

Book Title

Book Title

Student booklets are available via the QR code at the end of the book

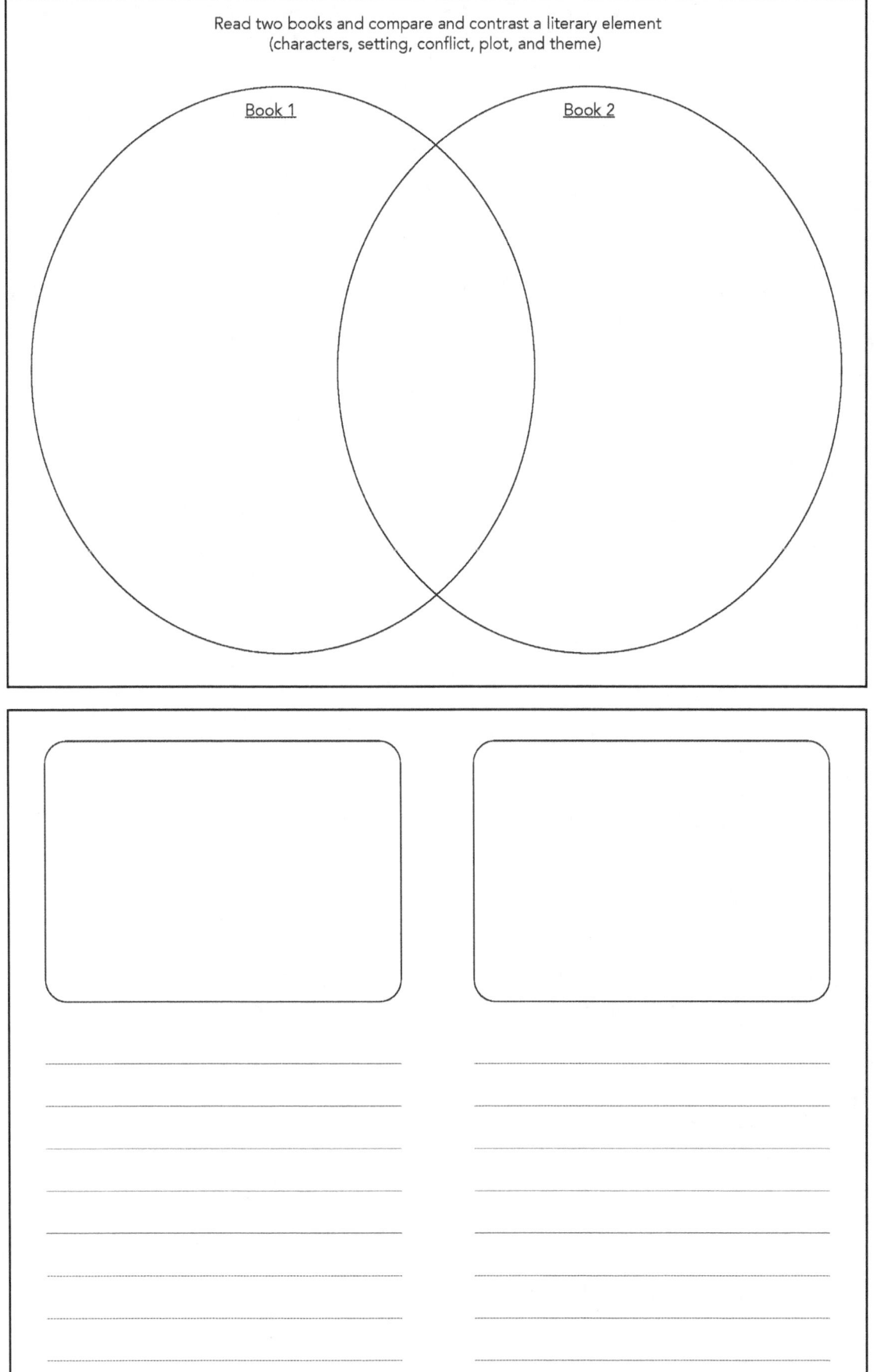

Read two books and compare and contrast a literary element
(characters, setting, conflict, plot, and theme)

Book 1

Book 2

Student booklets are available via the QR code at the end of the book

Book Title

Book Title

Title of Book One

Title of Book Two

Student booklets are available via the QR code at the end of the book

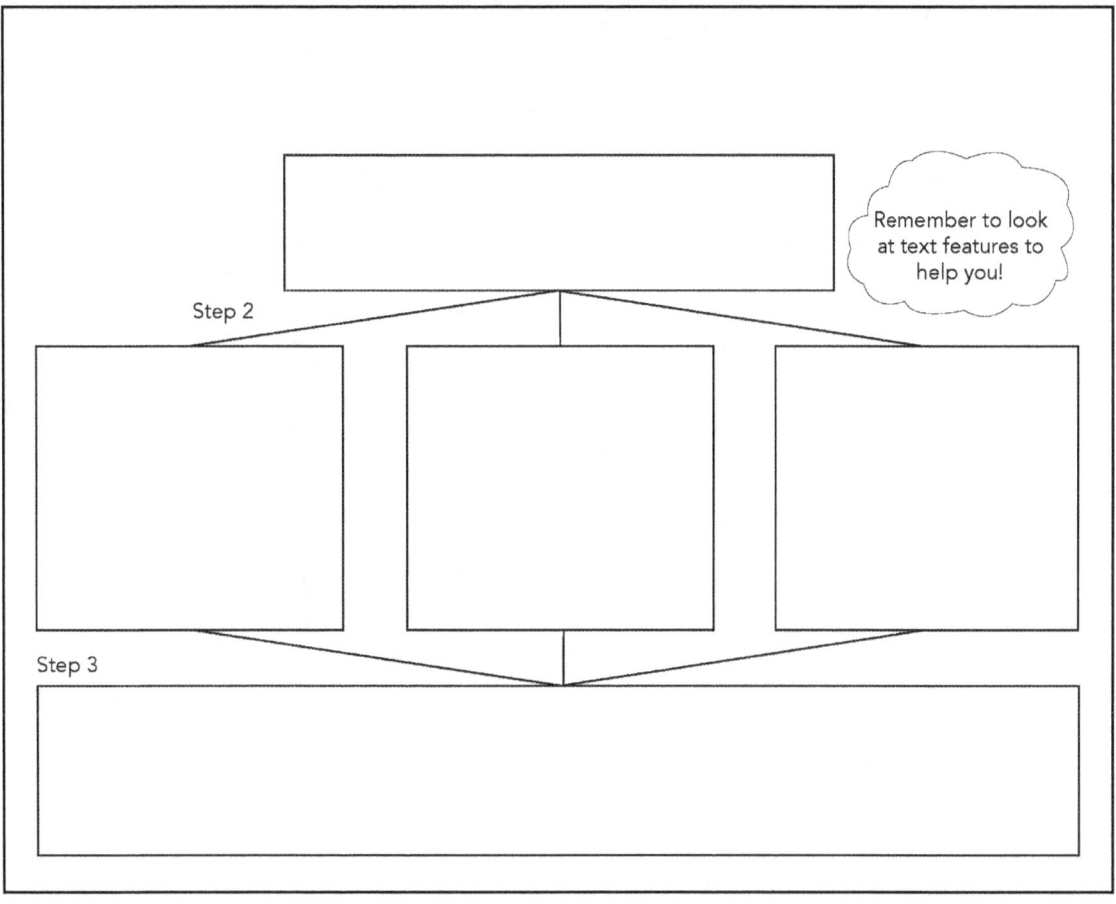

Step 2

Remember to look at text features to help you!

Step 3

Student booklets are available via the QR code at the end of the book

STUDENT BOOKLET DOWNLOAD

Purchasers of **How to Create Language Experts with Literary Terms** may use this QR code to download booklets from this book at no extra cost. This will ease the process of making copies for students and expand learning options. Both the print and digital download versions of this material are protected by copyright laws.

QR codes can be found in all LtoJ books, providing access to digital downloads of student worksheets.

ABOUT THE AUTHORS

Codi Hrouda grew up in the small town of Hubbard, Nebraska. After completing high school, Codi went on to pursue her degree in Elementary Education at Wayne State College, and graduated with a BA in Elementary Education in 2000.

Once graduated, Codi accepted her first job at Thurston Elementary School, in Thurston, Nebraska, as a fifth and sixth grade combination teacher. A year later, she and her husband moved to Columbus, Nebraska where she taught a year of first grade and then thirteen years of fourth grade at Centennial Elementary School. While teaching full-time in Columbus, she completed her master's degree in Curriculum and Instruction through Wayne State College. She graduated with her master's degree in May of 2006.

In 2014, Codi and her husband moved their family back to the area where she grew up to raise their three daughters. Codi accepted a fifth grade position at Dakota City Elementary in Dakota City, Nebraska where she continues to teach today. She just completed her twenty-second year of teaching in 2022. Codi spends her free time attending her daughters' activities, decorating, reading, and spending time with her family and friends.

Emma McInerney grew up in the small town of Elk Point, South Dakota. After completing high school, Emma went on to pursue a degree in healthcare at South Dakota State University (SDSU).

In 2015, she realized she was ready for a career change because her passion lies in education. She transferred to Dakota State University (DSU), earned a degree in Elementary Education, and graduated in 2019. Emma began her first job at Dakota City Elementary, in Dakota City, Nebraska, as a fifth grade teacher. While teaching full-time she completed her Masters degree in Curriculum and Instruction through Wayne State College, graduating in May of 2022. Emma concluded her third year of teaching in 2022, and she continues to teach alongside her co-author, Codi Hrouda.

Emma returned to her hometown of Elk Point after graduating, and spends her free time reading, gardening, and spending time with her boyfriend, family, and friends.

Dr. Lyle Lee Jenkins is an author, speaker, and recognized authority in improving educational outcomes. He believes that implementing a growth mindset and celebrating progress are the keys to helping students learn more and retain their enthusiasm for school.

His education experience, that spans over 50 years, ranges from working as a teacher, a principal, and a school superintendent in the California School System to being a University Professor. In 2003, Lyle Lee founded LtoJ, LLC hoping to impact and guide the way we approach education.

Lyle Lee Jenkins has authored six books showcasing continuous improvement in schools, including *How to Create a Perfect School*, *Optimize Your School*, *Permission to Forget*, *From Systems Thinking to Systemic Action*, *Improving Student Learning*, and *How to Create a Perfect Home School*. All literature offers powerful, practical suggestions for every aspect of education. The two most influential people supporting Dr. Jenkins's work are W. Edwards Deming and John Hattie.

Having spoken to educators all across the United States, Latin America, Europe, Australia, and Asia, Lyle Lee Jenkins is passionate about equipping the next generation with a true love of learning.

Dr. Lyle Lee Jenkins holds a Bachelor of Arts degree from Point Loma Nazarene University, a Masters of Education from San Jose State University and a Ph.D. from the Claremont Graduate University.

Lyle Lee Jenkins's website, www.LtoJ.net, is a great place to discover useful tools to guide your educational journey.

Do you have a great photo or video of your student using one of our products?

We would love the opportunity to share it on our website and social media channels!

Email us at info@ltoj.net

If you have a story to share, we would also like to hear from you. We feature student stories during presentations and on our social media accounts.

Our team loves sharing the joy of a child understanding new concepts. It allows our audience to experience firsthand the mission our team works towards every day; for students to maintain the same love of learning they brought to Kindergarten throughout all their years of schooling and into adulthood.

Thank you for being a loyal customer. We appreciate you!

The LtoJ Team

Follow us on Instagram, Facebook, TikTok and YouTube
@LtoJLLC

www.ingramcontent.com/pod-product-compliance
Lightning Source LLC
Chambersburg PA
CBHW081010120626
46546CB00010B/3087